LIVING IN A CALM COUNTRY

Peter Porter

Peter Porter

LIVING IN A CALM
COUNTRY

LONDON
OXFORD UNIVERSITY PRESS
NEW YORK   TORONTO
1975

Oxford University Press, Ely House, London W.1

GLASGOW NEW YORK TORONTO MELBOURNE WELLINGTON
CAPE TOWN IBADAN NAIROBI DAR ES SALAAM LUSAKA ADDIS ABABA
DELHI BOMBAY CALCUTTA MADRAS KARACHI LAHORE DACCA
KUALA LUMPUR SINGAPORE HONG KONG TOKYO

ISBN 0 19 211854 4

© *Oxford University Press* 1975

PRINTED IN GREAT BRITAIN
BY THE BOWERING PRESS PLYMOUTH

In Memoriam S.J.H. (1933–1974)

CONTENTS

ACKNOWLEDGEMENTS

ACKNOWLEDGEMENTS are due to the editors of the
following periodicals in which some of these poems first
appeared : *Ambit, The Critical Quarterly, Encounter,
The Listener, London Magazine, The New Review, New
Statesman, Overland, Poetry Nation, Pointer, Second Aeon,*
and *Wave. Exit, Pursued by a Bear* was commissioned by the
Globe Playhouse Trust for the Shakespeare Birthday
Celebrations at Southwark in April 1974. *An American
Military Cemetery in Tuscany* was included in my pamphlet,
A Share of the Market, published by *Honest Ulsterman*
publications, Belfast, 1973. Acknowledgements are also due to
the BBC in whose programmes some other poems were first
heard.

THE POETRY BOOK SOCIETY

105 Piccadilly, London WIV OAU

Selectors, Choices, Recommendations and Publications

Selectors 1954-74

Dannie Abse, J. R. Ackerley, W. H. Auden, Thomas Blackburn, Alan Brownjohn, Nevill Coghill, Cyril Connolly, Patric Dickinson, Martin Dodsworth, T. F. Eagleton, Ian Fletcher, G. S. Fraser, John Fuller, Roy Fuller, J. C. Hall, Michael Hamburger, Ian Hamilton, Christopher Hassall, John Hayward, John Holloway, Ted Hughes, Frank Kermode, Philip Larkin, Naomi Lewis, Karl Miller, Edwin Muir, Gabriel Pearson, James Reeves, V. Sackville-West, Janet Adam Smith, Terence Tiller, Anthony Thwaite, Vernon Watkins, David Wright.

Recent Choices

1965	Sylvia Plath	*Ariel*	Faber
	Roy Fuller	*Buff*	Deutsch
	John Holloway	*Wood and Windfall*	Routledge
	Kathleen Raine	*The Hollow Hill*	Hamish Hamilton
1966	Charles Tomlinson	*American Scenes and other poems*	Oxford
	Brian Higgins	*The Northern Fiddler*	Methuen
	Norman MacCaig	*Surroundings*	Chatto
	Peter Redgrove	*The Force and other poems*	Routledge and Kegan Paul
1967	Austin Clarke	*Old-Fashioned Pilgrimage*	Dolmen Press and Oxford
	John Fuller	*The Tree that Walked*	Chatto
	Thom Gunn	*Touch*	Faber
	Anthony Hecht	*The Hard Hours*	Oxford
1968	Charles Causley	*Underneath the Water*	Macmillan
	Roy Fuller	*New Poems*	Deutsch
	Derek Mahon	*Night-Crossing*	Oxford
	R. S. Thomas	*Not That He Brought Flowers*	Hart-Davis

1969	Peter Whigham	*The Blue-Winged Bee*	Anvil
	Seamus Heaney	*Door Into The Dark*	Faber
	Douglas Dunn	*Terry Street*	Faber
	David Holbrook	*Old World, New World*	Rapp & Whiting
1970	W. S. Graham	*Malcolm Mooney's Land*	Faber
	Ian Hamilton	*The Visit*	Faber
	Peter Porter	*The Last of England*	Oxford
	Elizabeth Jennings	*Lucidities*	Macmillan
1971	Thom Gunn	*Moly*	Faber
	Geoffrey Hill	*Mercian Hymns*	Deutsch
	Sylvia Plath	*Winter Trees*	Faber
	Gavin Ewart	*The Gavin Ewart Show*	Trigram
1972	William Plomer	*Celebrations*	Cape
	D. J. Enright	*Daughters of Earth*	Chatto
	Norman Nicholson	*A Local Habitation*	Faber
	Stewart Conn	*An Ear to the Ground*	Hutchinson
1973	John Smith	*Entering Rooms*	Chatto
	Edwin Morgan	*From Glasgow to Saturn*	Carcanet
	Michael Burn	*Out on a Limb*	Chatto
	Alasdair Maclean	*From the Wilderness*	Gollancz
1974	Geoffrey Holloway	*Rhine Jump*	L.M.E.
	Douglas Dunn	*Love or Nothing*	Faber
	Charles Tomlinson	*The Way In*	Oxford
	Andrew Waterman	*Living Room*	Marvell P.

Recent Recommendations

1965	David Gascoyne	*Collected Poems*	Oxford
	Norman MacCaig	*Measures*	Chatto & Windus
	David Wright	*Adam at Evening*	Hodder & Stoughton
	George Barker	*The True Confession of George Barker*	MacGibbon & Kee
	D. J. Enright	*The Old Adam*	Chatto & Windus
1965	George MacBeth	*A Doomsday Book*	Scorpion Press
	Paul Dehn	*The Fern on the Rock*	Hamish Hamilton
	John Heath-Stubbs	*Selected Poems*	Oxford
	John Smith	*A Discreet Immorality*	Hart-Davis
	C. Day Lewis	*The Room*	Cape
	Christopher Middleton	*Nonsequences*	Longmans
1966	Ruth Pitter	*Still by Choice*	Cresset Press
	A. K. Ramanujan	*The Striders*	Oxford
	Anne Halley	*Between Wars*	Oxford
	James K. Baxter	*Pig Island Letters*	Oxford
	Edward Brathwaite	*Rights of Passage*	Oxford
	Louis Zukofsky	*'A' 1-12*	Cape

1967	Geoffrey Grigson	*A Skull in Salop*	Macmillan
	Elizabeth Jennings	*Collected Poems*	Macmillan
	Thomas Kinsella	*Nightwalker*	Dolmen Press
1968	Tony Connor	*Kon in Springtime*	Oxford
	Austin Clarke	*The Echo at Coole*	Dolmen Press
	Geoffrey Hill	*King Log*	Deutsch
	Richard Murphy	*The Battle of Aughrim*	Faber
	Barry Cole	*Moonsearch*	Methuen
1969	Geoffrey Grigson	*Ingestion of Ice-Cream*	Macmillan
	David Harsent	*A Violent Country*	Oxford
1970	Glyn Hughes	*Neighbours*	Macmillan
	Hugo Williams	*Sugar Daddy*	Oxford
	John Montague	*Tides*	Dolmen Press
1971	Roy Fisher	*Matrix*	Fulcrum
	Jon Silkin	*Amana Grass*	Chatto
	John Cotton	*Old Movies*	Chatto
	Kathleen Raine	*The Lost Country*	Dolmen
	Molly Holden	*Air and Chill Earth*	Chatto
	X. J. Kennedy	*Breaking and Entering*	Oxford
	W. R. Rodgers	*Collected Poems*	Oxford
1972	Anne Ridler	*Some Time After*	Faber
	Alan Brownjohn	*Warrior's Career*	Macmillan
	Iain Crichton Smith	*Love Poems and Elegies*	Gollancz
	Wayne Brown	*On the Coast*	Deutsch
	Charles Tomlinson	*Written on Water*	Oxford
1973	Norman MacCaig	*The White Bird*	Chatto
	J. C. Hall	*A House of Voices*	Chatto
	James K. Baxter	*Runes*	Oxford
	Lawrence Durrell	*Vega*	Faber
1974	Jon Stallworthy	*Hand In Hand*	Chatto
	Brian Jones	*For Mad Mary*	L.M.E.
	George Kendrick	*Bicycle Tyre in a Tall Tree*	Carcanet

Bulletins

Bulletins, containing contributions from the authors chosen and recommended, and poems by the recommended author are sent out with each quarter's Choice. Where back numbers of the Bulletins are still in print, they are available price 5p.

Recent Poetry Supplements (Price 13p each)

1964   *Poetry Supplement dedicated to the memory of Joseph Compton 1891-1964. Ed.* Roy Fuller.
Contributors: Nissim Ezekiel, John Fuller, Francis Hope, P. J. Kavanagh, Peter Levi, Hugo Williams.

1965   *Poetry Supplement. Ed.* Francis Hope.
Contributors: Fleur Adcock, Martin Bell, Gavin Ewart, Seamus Heaney, Susanne Knowles, Douglas Livingstone, Peter Porter, Stevie Smith, Ted Walker.

1966   *Poems. Ed.* Eric W. White.
Contributors: W. H. Auden, George Barker, Jack Clemo, Harry Fainlight, David Jones, Richard Murphy, Norman Nicholson, Brian Patten, Tom Pickard, Edgell Rickword, Vernon Watkins, Sheila Wingfield.

1967   *Twelve Poets. Ed.* Charles Osborne.
Contributors: Edward Brathwaite, Marcus Cumberledge, Gavin Ewart, Louise Gluck, Harry Guest, Michael Levey, George MacBeth, Matthew Mead, Peter Porter, Vernon Scannell, Nikos Stangos, Hugo Williams.

1968   *Eight Poets. Ed.* Ian Hamilton.
Contributors: Alan Brownjohn, Donald Davie, Colin Falck, Michael Fried, John Fuller, David Harsent, Anthony Thwaite, Jon Stallworthy.

1969   *Poetry Supplement. Ed.* Martin Dodsworth.
Contributors: Barry Cole, Donald Davie, Douglas Dunn, Gavin Ewart, Geoffrey Grigson, Ian Hamilton, David Holbrook, Alan Ross.

1970   *Poetry Supplement. Ed.* John Fuller.
Contributors: Alastair Fowler, Ian Hamilton, David Harsent, Glyn Hughes, Harold Massingham, Peter Porter, Peter Redgrove, Biron Walker.

1971   *Poetry Supplement. Ed.* Terry Eagleton.
Contributors: John Barrell, Douglas Dunn, John Fuller, Michael Hamburger, Seamus Heaney, Jon Silkin, James Simmons, Ted Walker.

1972   *Thirteen Poets. Ed.* Dannie Abse.
Contributors: Thomas Blackburn, Alan Brownjohn, Stewart Conn, Douglas Dunn, D. J. Enright, William Meredith, Peter Porter, Jeremy Robson, M. L. Rosenthal, Vernon Scannell, Jon Stallworthy, Adrian Stokes, Anthony Thwaite.

1973   *New Poems 1973. Ed.* Charles Osborne.
Contributors: Charles Causley, Kevin Crossley-Holland, D. J. Enright, Anthony Howell, Peter Jay, George MacBeth, Tom Raworth, Alan Ross, Vernon Scannell, Stephen Spender, Eric W. White.

1974   *Poetry Supplement. Ed.* Philip Larkin. Price 40p.
Contributors: Joan Barton, Patricia Beer, Alan Brownjohn, Robert Conquest, Douglas Dunn, D. J. Enright, Gavin Ewart, Roy Fisher, Roy Fuller, J. C. Hall, John Hewitt, Molly Holden, Elizabeth Jennings, Philip Larkin, George MacBeth, Roger McGough, Edwin Morgan, Brian Patten, Peter Porter, Vernon Scannell, Jon Stallworthy, Anthony Thwaite, John Wain.

Check Lists of New Verse (Price 13p each)

These lists are available for each year from 1957

Holograph Poems

Edmund Blunden: *A Hong Kong House* (50p)

The John Roberts Press, London

What it is and does

THE POETRY BOOK SOCIETY

The Poetry Book Society, founded in 1954, is non-profit-making, and is helped financially by the Arts Council of Great Britain. Membership costs £5 per year and brings post free the following:

1. A book of new poetry every quarter.

2. With the book, the Society's Bulletin with contributions from the authors of the books chosen and recommended.

3. A special Poetry Supplement at Christmas. (2 copies)

4. A yearly check list of books of new verse.

The Choice

The quarterly book of poetry is chosen for members by Selectors appointed every year by the Society's Board of Management. It is always a book of new poems. During the Society's existence some of the most interesting poetry of the day has come to members on publication.

The Recommendations

The Selectors also recommend, every quarter, any other books of special merit. The recommendations are announced in the Society's Bulletin which also prints specimen poems from them or unpublished poems by their authors. In addition to books of new poems, volumes of collected poems and anthologies of contemporary poetry are eligible for recommendation (but not for choice).

Advantages

Since a subscription costs no more than the published price of the books members receive, an obvious benefit is derived from membership. In addition a member knows that the book he receives has been carefully selected by experts, usually practising poets or critics.

It need hardly be said that the Society serves the needs of organisations such as schools (many of which are in membership) as well as those of individuals, since one result of continued membership is the building up of a representative library of the best modern verse.

There are hidden advantages too: the Society's existence certainly encourages publishers to publish books of new poetry and to keep their price to the minimum. To become a member of the Society is a practical way of helping the art and dissemination of poetry.

Poetry Festivals

The Society promotes an annual festival of international poetry each summer in London. Advance details are supplied to all members.

How to join the Society

Either A Fill in the Order Form opposite and send with a remittance to the address below

Or B Fill in the Banker's Order Form opposite and send it to the address below

The Secretary
The Poetry Book Society Limited
105 Piccadilly
London WIV OAU

A. Poetry Book Society   *Order Form*

Please enrol me as a member of the Poetry Book Society for
*this/next calendar year at a cost of £5 or its equivalent in foreign
currency. For bona fide students the rate is £3.50 or its equiva-
lent in foreign currency.

  *(1) My cheque is enclosed   *(2) Please send me a bill

Name Mr/Mrs/Miss† ....

Address (in full) † ....

....

Date..

            **Delete as applicable*   † *Block Letters please*

B. Poetry Book Society   *Banker's Order*

To...
(Name of Bank)

....
(Address of Bank)

Please pay to the account of The Poetry Book Society Limited
(A/C No. 46707440) at Messrs. Coutts and Company, 440 Strand,
London, W.C.2. (Clearing code 18-00-02) the sum of............................
due on.. (date of payment)
and pay a similar sum on January 1st of each succeeding year
until further notice.

Name Mr/Mrs/Miss...

Address (in full) ....

....

Date...

              (Signed) ....

'*I have always held firmly that a nation which ceases to produce poetry will in the long run cease to be able to enjoy and even understand the great poetry of its own past.*'

T. S. ELIOT, O.M.,
speaking at a press conference held by
the Poetry Book Society, 10 April 1956.

AT THE CASTLE HOTEL, TAUNTON

Today it's not scones but tea-cakes
    (And the sound of ambulances
    in the reconstructed streets)—

Rich voices are discussing the new Warden
    (The Show is the best for years,
    the architects' watercolours outstanding)—

Pearls and brogues survive, cashmere clings
    (Is this the Ark of Adultery
    or two old friends killing time?)—

Interlopers must wait for their tea
    (There's only one waitress on today,
    her footsteps are masked on the stairs)—

Hands want something to do, eyes won't idle
    (*Country Life* in a rexine folder :
    who buys, who sells all these houses?)—

O impossible England under the modern stars
    (Mr. Edward du Cann thanks the voters
    of Taunton for their generous support)—

So much beauty, so unexpectedly preserved
    (And we two strangers have today
    honoured gentle Eliot at East Coker)—

Not only the pheasant eating by the road
    (And the cider factory, the industrial
    archaeology with the rural)—

But the pattern of beauty changing in the air
    (Fields painted by history, a steam
    of seasons softening what lives)—

Somerset for survivors and a good thing too
(Seventeenth-century farm house,
part-converted, owner abroad)—

Seen from Ilminster spire, everything is safe
(It is being kept for posterity
but where do the people of England live?)

HIS AND HERS

Mornings weaving through the mud
Gave his high boots a cracked glory,
And she, crying where she stood,
Heard the hardly bothered-with story;
Each not knowing that pain clings
To the cleaned surface of things.

The greenhouse overspored with seeds
And the motor mower dried of oil,
Over the garage virginia creeper bleeds,
The lawn has patches of bare soil—
This is the Estate Agent's concern
Since he's in a box and she in an urn.

Behind a door missed by visitors
High boots and binoculars stand—
The arrogance his, the unhappiness hers;
Neither can get the upper hand,
The doing and the watching part
Outliving the torments of the heart.

ANGER

In long lines
about the hill, crops are at war
with evening

The moon high,
glimpsed then gone,
a drift of upper leaves
in the dark wind of Cornwall

To give no part
of oneself to death
before the time

Only to sit
with one's back to music
and no forgiveness

Colouring
the air and scattering
flakes of fury

LIVING IN A CALM COUNTRY

Each picture is a comic strip condensed.
You stare at Santa Fina on her bench
And the palisades are packed—
Looking is locking up, eyes are a fence.

A change of element to wallow in!
The swimmer wades through words—to him
Come doves and office pigeons,
Tu quoqueing his music, pinking his skin.

The difference is (again) the fact of time,
Such a lovely word that rhymes with rhyme :
Pictures stand still and still
Music composes the world, poems set lines.

Living in a calm country which is me
Is not like architecture or the sea
Or diligence of diction or
Any Mixolydian matter, it's green, grey, green.

Then back to Santa Fina who gave up
Her life by giving up her seat, the luck
Of those the gods love, unlike
Myself at the window now, calm as a cup.

Playing with selfishness, I propose
Rules for the game, the most outrageous clothes
On truth, a cunning heart
Pumping in praise of time, as the world goes.

ODE TO AFTERNOON

A command to the middle-aged,
you shall write disguised love poems
so that the young may respect you
when the truth is known

They will ensex your abstracts,
wink knowingly at all
the stale erudition
which so enrages your critics

You must make capital out of despair :
real pain is never art,
turn instead to quotidian tasks,
Grub Street at the obsessional !

In your review of *The Romance of Linear B*,
notice that all the texts are Official Art,
the numbers of the king's combs and cattle—
their songs you must imagine for yourself

Of *The Eighteen Chorales*, there is much love of God—
you alone have cracked the cypher
and know what he meant when he told the soul
to bedeck itself for its bridegroom

In the middle of *The Children's Crusade*
you may put two adolescents under a tree
poking bits of bark down each other's front,
music by Puccini, the sun declining

Having set the scene, you are in the Land
of Afternoon. Sex, if it comes, will be late,
up some stairs following a nervous lunch,
her eyes like a Florentine postcard

In the afternoon they came unto a land
in which it seemed always afternoon:
The fathers were at the races
and the lawnmowers ran all over the hills

Afternoon men in the morning of the world,
we donate our three score and ten
to a beleaguered maturity—
province of afghan hounds and honeydew

Mother, the girls you warned me of
are waiting behind the rector's hedge,
I can hear their voices : they are content
with the usual menagerie

Home of averages where human kind
cannot bear very much reality
but the sun is always over the yardarm
and we are for the dark

Die Untergang des Abendlandes
is still a best seller though it sounds
better with a stierhorn's blast
than a song at twilight

These quotations will keep nobody warm,
so put away the deck chairs
and the half-finished poem
and return to your research

Which was into the lineaments
of great fiction, and began
with the motherless boy
circuiting his grown-up garden :

Huge tears are in the pond,
every hurt has a face like a flower—
that will be music across the road
from the long-dead birthday party

O sprays of scent and my blue aunts,
I am coming with my excuses ready :
I was reading down in the boatshed,
how shall we get through the afternoon?

GOOD VIBES
For Shena Mackay

If you hadn't noticed the unprominent sign
We'd have missed Adlestrop, missed the gone
Railway and the bullock raking his back
In the hollow holly-bower. Missed, too, the sky
So intolerably lofty in its beakered blue
And the loping dog which frightened me
(Which is how I know he was friendly)—
Most noticeably missed the station bench
And ADLESTROP, the railway sign, with Edward
Thomas's poem on a plaque for pilgrims.
Not a great poem, but rich in names
And heartache and certainly a focus for
A sinisterly fine October afternoon.
Down one lane adjacent the Home for Children,
(With what impediment we never found),
All the day-labourers of Oxfordshire and Gloucestershire
Were about their honey-making masonry
Of Cotswold stone, and the bullocks were nifty
In the meadow by the creek. There were no
Devils in the landscape, exhalations from
Ponds and dogs' breath and graveyards after rain
Could only be imagined in such unexpected sunshine,
But we felt them, felt a new humidity,
Oppressive like the self. This was a short halt
On two pilgrimages, a look-back out of Hades,
Such as the gods provide for laughter in their
Chronicles. Yet that sound, that risible division,
Strikes mortal earth some otherwise—such as
Gravel flicking from a low-slung bumper,
A trailing jet above, a jostling on the eaves
Of sycamores. It was as if the well-intentioned
Dead were breathing out and blessing everyone,
Vibrations of the minute, without franchise,

A pointless benediction. Thinking again, I feel
Grateful that you saw through uncleaned windows
A name which meant the same to all half-educated
Persons. To have trod on ground in happiness
Is to be shaken by the true immortals.

SEASIDE PICNIC

Here where sprawl the armed persuaders,
    Denizens of three-inch oceans
    Who rage as Genghis over sand and rock
    Ignoring only the anemone's motions,
    Its meatless, beautiful tick-tock;
Here, scaled down from the world of waders,

Whose holiday gingerliness is as remote
    As God, the relentless law
    Renews itself : the soft-backed crab
    Ventures too far from its lodge, and claw
    And life both break at one stab
Of an old need and like seaweed are left to float.

This terror is enacted in seventy pools
    Of a single rock till the tide
    Renews like Deucalion's advance
    Another flood of darkness, and to hide
    Is the victim's and predator's equal chance.
This is a world without self-doubters or fools,

Egregiously unlike the pretty playground
    Of its kindhearted great
    Who might say to a clambering child
    'Don't leave that sea-snail to its fate
    But right it on its shelf so the mild
Worm can cling, the life platform be sound.'

For they are swayed by such overreaching waters
    As they do not recognize
    Along the bristling beach on afternoons
    Of sun, and having learned to prize
    Hope, pass each other plates and spoons,
Unpacking love for their murderous sons and daughters.

11

TO MAKE IT REAL

After having written verses in tight corsets,
verses inspired by German Idealism
and random, thin, self-justifying verses,
I feel the need to trap a piece of real.
I started the trochaic motor up
some lines before but now I slip the clutch—
trochees and iambs are so Janus-faced,
I leave our virtuosi of the Classics
to startle us with Choriambs and Sapphics.

Despair might get some music into this,
poetry must do up its own laces.
Somewhere beyond my window (shall we say
in Pessary, Ohio) a widowed lady
rocks like acacia fragrance in the night
and lets a naked light bulb close her eyes,
the neighbour's dog her psychopomp, the
ruttish evening full of floating dust
as she is candled inwards, yet not fussed.

I made this lady up : my cat ascends
the curtain wildly clawing till she falls;
non sequiturs of heartburn and despair
are felt like persons in the early dark.
My mortal lady with the finished eyes
will not be named and will not need a grave,
but for her benediction London kneels—
our well-lit world goes in the Word Machine,
chaff in the jaws of God, blood in a dream.

THE STORY OF MY CONVERSION

I have begun to live in a new land,
not the old land of fear
but the new one of disappointment.

At 45 I am at the right age
to appreciate that my new country
enjoys good relations with death.

But I am also returning to the surprises
of childhood, the sun-slatted boredom,
castles of the kingdom of bananas.

Not me, Lord. The summons is not for me,
I am considering my student's albums,
girls' addresses, hours of drinking, anger.

A marvellous mustiness surrounds me;
The Book of Useless Knowledge in my hand,
I salute the thousand green horrors, the self.

In the Eighteen Eighties, Freud
applied for a job in a Bendigo hospital—
it's enough to make Tasman miss the boat.

Nothing is alike in my familiar world.
The boy of the unwritten journal
would get my prig's sneer. Good God, his prose!

If he had a cypher for things not done
he'd write *halek* for the Greek girl
who went to the same Communion classes.

I might have been born in Galicia,
in the poet-killing provinces:
the olives look to me outside Cortona.

Instead, my vote went to verandahs.
What has this to do with the land
of disappointment? A style, or lack of style.

I am fond of the overdone. Of Luca Signorelli
and Castagno. I'll never learn simplicity,
I don't feel things strongly. I was never young.

I asked my friends how they swallowed the world.
They said, you will only learn by doing it.
That's why I would sooner be asleep.

I must use passive verbs. Describe death
as matter being re-cycled. I feel like someone
in a German play winding up the moon.

But this new land I was talking about—
it has a vocation for mad creatures,
they live by arguing with the sea.

I, too, am licensed to produce a masterpiece.
I start: 'In the Eighteen Eighties, Freud applied
for a doctor's job in Bendigo—or was it Ballarat?'

NIGHT CROSSING

The old charm dies hard, the vicious moon
A yellow mango and the ferryman saying
Some oblationary rune above the rising flood;
Night and silence have always been indoors,
A provincial pinchbeck still extraordinary
Among the duodecimo principalities
And me the hidalgo of all self-esteem.

I listen to the Time-travelling Schoolmistress :
Avoid simplicity, she says, that
Shakespearean gold made of short words.
You are a tyro of untrusted syllables
And your pretence of knowledge comes out
As dreams, like these, distorted, polychromed,
All about sex but more of neaps than nipples.

He comes closer daily, the white-winged visitor
With his pouch of riddles. If we stand close
To the bar and swear undying friendship, he may
Go away. It's just another reconnaissance
As is this life which Shelley said
Stains the white radiance et cetera—
I won't die young to make my language work.

But I am haunted, not by books or notes,
But by disparate refuse of a species' mind.
Where the diamonds of our race show clear
Light from the Father, I fudge murky red :
I go to sleep to greet the myths, pure comic-strip
With serious charges following, father and mother's blood
Upon the always shamed and always bachelor sheets.

Never to be what I say as never to know,
For instance, if the ferryman will be the same

Across the river, or whether a voice reading
COSMO MEDICI MAGNO ETRURIA DUCI
Is my old headmaster or the floating oracle
They promised me when I renounced my love
To become a good resentful husband.

The questions the Customs ask are quite unclassical,
The names unknown to Pope or Plutarch—
Some words this hand will try to set in place
Changing the mixed-up facts to meet the case.
In the bright morning of night I pay my way
Into the Great Exhibition : from here on
The gods are dead, I meet their proud originals.

FAMILY ALBUM

Tenable in dreams, here they are twice
as plausible, holding court to the lens,
with nothing to say but the truth.
      Myself, my mother,
culled from the caucus of summer
by a relative's whim : how did the fat woman
keep so many bees off her howling son?
      That man, chained to
his gross watch, wearing his waistcoat
like Prometheus his rock, did he edge
to the aerodrome to show he was too
frightened to enter the twentieth century?
      It makes a good fiction
to leer at their confidence. Something else
would fit in. The light, acid but milky,
along the near shore and the ironclad ferry
touching the stage; Cousin Timperley
walking an ice cream up to the pines,
Beethoven for supper, everyone upright.
      Later, dispersal may offer
your motorcade stopping en route to Tiberias,
'This is Cana, so don't check the water
in your radiator'. Over us looms Mount
Gilboa where Saul fell on his sword,
a mortar lob from the red hibiscus
kibbutz, its blond children playing
through the collective afternoon.
      Pictures from a lost
exhibition. Not the pianola and
the telescope, but a high-backed
Russian chair and the brilliantined
bridegroom asleep after venery.
Or this tribute : 'How we brought

the Good News', key of F Minor,
the house in the corn.

        That hand, that brown face,
now papery, channelled with heart
disease, the transit of Venus.
Mother and father met here in me
ascribing a terror of photographs
to the lingering snake in the garden.

        Made objective now
on the lake where the red-eyed fish
walk on wallpaper. O sails of death
that we watched on the river, weeks of rain
when we came to our father's house,
the pictures are ready, shall we walk in?

AN AUSTRALIAN GARDEN
For Sally Lehmann

Here we enact the opening of the world
And everything that lives shall have a name
To show its heart; there shall be Migrants,
Old Believers, Sure Retainers; the cold rose
Exclaim perfection to the gangling weeds,
The path lead nowhere—this is like entering
One's self, to find the map of death
Laid out untidily, a satyr's grin
Signalling 'You are here' : tomorrow
They are replanting the old court,
Puss may be banished from the sun-warmed stone.

See how our once-lived lives stay on to haunt us,
The flayed beautiful limbs of childhood
In the bole and branches of a great angophora—
Here we can climb and sit on memory
And hear the words which death was making ready
From the start. Such talking as the trees attempt
Is a lesson in perfectability. It stuns
The currawongs along the breaks of blue—
Their lookout cries have guarded Paradise
Since the expulsion of the heart, when man,
Bereft of joy, turned his red hand to gardens.

Spoiled Refugees nestle near Great Natives;
A chorus of winds stirs the pagoda'd stamens :
In this hierarchy of miniatures
Someone is always leaving for the mountains,
Civil servant ants are sure the universe
Stops at the hard hibiscus; the sun is drying
A beleaguered snail and the hydra-headed
Sunflowers wave like lights. If God were to plant
Out all His hopes, He'd have to make two more

19

Unknown Lovers, ready to find themselves
In innocence, under the weight of His green ban.

In the afternoon we change—an afterthought,
Those deeper greens which join the stalking shadows—
The lighter wattles look like men of taste
With a few well-tied leaves to brummel-up
Their poise. Berries dance in a southerly wind
And the garden tide has turned. Dark on dark.
Janus leaves are opening to the moon
Which makes its own grave roses. Old Man
Camellias root down to keep the sun intact,
The act is canopied with stars. A green sea
Rages through the landscape all the night.

We will not die at once. Nondescript pinks
Survive the death of light and over-refined
Japanese petals bear the weight of dawn's first
Insect. An eye makes damask on the dew.
Time for strangers to accustom themselves
To habitat. What should it be but love?
The transformations have been all to help
Unmagical creatures find their proper skins,
The virgin and the leonine. The past's a warning
That the force of joy is quite unswervable—
'Out of this wood do not desire to go.'

In the sun, which is the garden's moon, the barefoot
Girl espies her monster, all his lovely specialty
Like hairs about his heart. The dream is always
Midday and the two inheritors are made
Proprietors. They have multiplied the sky.
Where is the water, where the terraces, the Tritons
And the cataracts of moss? This is Australia
And the villas are laid out inside their eyes :
It would be easy to unimagine everything,
Only the pressure made by love and death
Holds up the bodies which this Eden grows.

ON FIRST LOOKING INTO
CHAPMAN'S HESIOD

For 5p at a village fête I bought
Old Homer-Lucan who popped Keats's eyes,
Print smaller than the Book of Common Prayer
But Swinburne at the front, whose judgement is
Always immaculate. I'll never read a tenth
Of it in what life I have left to me
But I did look at *The Georgics*, as he calls
The Works and Days, and there I saw, not quite
The view from Darien but something strange
And balking—Australia, my own country
And its edgy managers—in the picture of
Euboeaen husbandry, terse family feuds
And the minds of gods tangential to the earth.

Like a Taree smallholder splitting logs
And philosophizing on his dangling billies,
The poet mixes hard agrarian instances
With sour sucks to his brother. Chapman, too,
That perpetual motion poetry machine,
Grinds up the classics like bone meal from
The abbatoirs. And the same blunt patriotism,
A long-winded, emphatic, kelpie yapping
About our land, our time, our fate, our strange
And singular way of moons and showers, lakes
Filling oddly—yes, Australians are Boeotians,
Hard as headlands, and, to be fair, with days
As robust as the Scythian wind on stone.

To teach your grandmother to suck eggs
Is a textbook possibility in New South Wales
Or outside Ascra. And such a genealogy too!
The Age of Iron is here, but oh the memories
Of Gold—pioneers preaching to the stringybarks,

Boring the land to death with verses and with
Mental Homes. 'Care-flying ease' and 'Gift-
devouring kings' become the Sonata of the Shotgun
And Europe's Entropy; for 'the axle-tree, the quern,
The hard, fate-fostered man' you choose among
The hand castrator, kerosene in honey tins
And mystic cattlemen: the Land of City States
Greets Australia in a farmer's gods.

Hesiod's father, caught in a miserable village,
Not helped by magic names like Helicon,
Sailed to improve his fortunes, and so did
All our fathers—in turn, their descendants
Lacked initiative, other than the doctors' daughters
Who tripped to England. Rough-nosed Hesiod
Was sure of his property to a slip-rail—
Had there been grants, he'd have farmed all
Summer and spent winter in Corinth
At the Creative Writing Class. Chapman, too,
Would vie with Steiner for the Pentecostal
Silver Tongue. Some of us feel at home nowhere,
Others in one generation fuse with the land.

I salute him then, the blunt old Greek whose way
Of life was as cunning as organic. His poet
Followers still make me feel déraciné
Within myself. One day they're on the campus,
The next in wide hats at a branding or
Sheep drenching, not actually performing
But looking the part and getting instances
For odes that bruise the blood. And history,
So interior a science it almost seems
Like true religion—who would have thought
Australia was the point of all that craft
Of politics in Europe? The apogee, it seems,
Is where your audience and its aspirations are.

'The colt, and mule, and horn-retorted steer'—
A good iambic line to paraphrase.
Long storms have blanched the million bones
Of the Aegean, and as many hurricanes
Will abrade the headstones of my native land :
Sparrows acclimatize but I still seek
The permanently upright city where
Speech is nature and plants conceive in pots,
Where one escapes from what one is and who
One was, where home is just a postmark
And country wisdom clings to calendars,
The opposite of a sunburned truth-teller's
World, haunted by precepts and the Pleiades.

FROGS AT LAGO DI BOLSENA

Having come down and run the car into sand
Not a foot from the reeds, the tense changes to
The Italian present and stories of Montefiascone
Are right for the first perambulation—
Only a few plastic bags floating and the smell
Of burning in the hills mild as eleven o'clock :
Then the frogs start – out there in the shallows, one
After another clamouring against official Nature.

For Nature is official here, its privilege extended
To recalcitrant weeds and momentous blossoms—
The Miracle of Bolsena struck from an open sky
And like a sunset the Host ran blood : what then
Can prevail upon the gentle waters, calm and bloodless,
When Christ's sanguinity fills the slaughterhouses
And the bone-dry churches? A corpse in damask
Holds the unsyntactical silence of despair.

Invisible and croaking in their plainness, the frogs
Speak of a similarly certain pain never
Lessening, and of the will to bring new pain
After, which this Italy has squared into art,
And which pilgrims with books in their hands try
To exorcize by long looks at lakes, judging
The far bank and marvellous islands until
The picture is captured and killed for their dreams.

AN AMERICAN MILITARY CEMETERY
IN TUSCANY

Why, I wonder, are there so few cows
Amid the succulent green of the tracks
And the neat, staked vine-plants in their rows?
This is the Chianti country,
The river mud a Helena Rubenstein pack
Ensuring through raging Summer a beauty
Of self-possession, a coolness waving back.

What appears a castle is a convent
Endowed by Florentine ambition, then
Comes the Winegrowers' Co-operative, meant
To look democratic and new—
Its striped blinds and sun-dazzled men
Wave to the tourist bus through thin blue
Exhaust bringing them dollars, marks and yen.

Because the land's flat for some miles
The bus keeps the cemetery in sight
For two miles at least—set like dials
For the eye of the deity
The headstones seem to the overbright
Travellers disagreeable presences—the laity
Find, as inside Santa Croce, God is uptight.

Underneath, men of Oregon and Minnesota
Are learning to be as green as Tuscany,
That dark green which has always had its quota
Of the most courageous blood—
Afterwards, a man can be tall as a pine tree
Straightening for the wind, or like flood
Water disperse himself in the silent majority.

As the bus passes this geometric field
A shiver runs from it to the sun :

Each of these innocent worlds is sealed
Under pressure of love and hate,
Each named soul is a precise no-one
Discovering the mystery too late,
It is not fulfilled, it is only done.

A TABLE OF COINCIDENCES

The map of self is a grid of crossroads—
The tanned garage attendant is also
The learned custodian of shards,
The unhelpful presider over a dozen
Phones stops your plane in time
To wing you back to love. They cross and cross,
The focus of care and the occasional nuisance,
The reed-stealer and the bald historian.
Lucky indeed to have a graveyard
In your head : walk by the wild hibiscus
Where an army vanished—through the haze
The low lake waves keep their tint of violence.

Even our rulers eat themselves to death.
A professor writes a book on the third period
Of his great composer; next door, the new genius
Creates relevant art with Woolworth balloons—
The solemn thinkers are the ones with hate.
The oracle's advice is to fake it well,
By which she means, learn to live with
Your imagination. You may desire universal
Love but your hand has obsession
In its curve. There is no Devil and perhaps
No God, but the walls are running blood
From the unsightly pictures of your dreams.

Still, every tomb requires two masks,
The slipping grin of terror and the running
Nose of irresponsibility. There, by the wand
Of magic, an Attic outline strokes its prick,
Hoping to come before the police arrive—
Better to face the dark with something to remember.
Stalled by the roses with your favourite uncle,
Thinking only of Dryden and the sinking

27

Of the *Emden,* you go to the universe
Of interchangeables—take this to heart!
The day Columbus discovered America
Was the day Piero della Francesca died.

Each wasted day lives on to waste tomorrow.
Three bitter seeds were put in Adam's grave
That the bright flags of history might unfurl.
The world is far away at this high window
Where jet trails chalk a pane of the cold sky.
'My bitter days do waste and I do languish'—
In the mirror I see the face of an old man
With a big nose; my daughter has dark
Celtic skin which shrivelled in the sun of death
When my mother wore it; the man on the path
Is our Hermes of the commercial smile;
Our plane is late, the courier calms our fears.

THAT DEPRESSION IS AN ABSTRACT

That depression is an abstract
is my doctor's view, who watches me open
one ear on a hinge and looks with interest
at a countryside of flowers and barges
and squares of green each carrying a cow—
        None of this is necessary
he says in his subtle lower case,
you have landlines to ten capitals.
        Good thinking,
bring the calabashes of iced wine
and the little sausages, I reply.
        Lie on this couch
and tell me what Europe said to you.
        She showed me an olive hillside
with the minty dead trowelled in a wall
and scented black steadying itself
for picnics on Mt. Erebus.
        She took my brown eyes
for gristle, something she could never swallow,
they had held tears at one age—
        She said, my son,
I would name a river for you
if only I had one left—
I loved your galloping through the evening fields,
your snout plating over and your gills
forming where the love-bites were.
        I saw the old castle
where deformity took itself as subject
and wrote God into the moon. Aunty Dolour
was my university and our good dog
played the Wolf of Gubbio
at the back door.
        Eventually, doctor,
we must come down to cases
but my memory is bad.

29

There are these polemics
you write against the new art—
'Why persecutest thou me?'
You have a cruel masterpiece
crying to get out, Saints Cosmas
and Damian healing a Rider
Haggard impi.
   Six pounds fifty
an hour should clear your head.
Indeed, as the sun stretched along my side,
I gazed at the advertisements—
   I do not feel depressed
although it is old in May and not
my time of year.
   I would like you
to use plain syntax and straight words
and to practise your left-hand scales!
   They fell from my eyes
in the first reels of eternity,
my bones were hollow before the lark's—
having paid and spoken and been listened to,
I have my certificate of going back,
guaranteeing it as it was then,
coming down a winding road of villas
to the Badia, the lodge gates plaqued
'Domenico Cimarosa lived here
in 1779', and then the black sky breaking,
seeing a face I loved and knowing
it had no respect for me, seeing my father
in the rain trying to clip the bougainvillea.
   Until death
the abstracts will have silver faces,
baroque lanterns like the moon,
terror pressed into depression,
   you and you and you,
father, son and lover of the world.

THE STORM

There where it's endless, it has this form of age,
of the feet no longer willing to enter
the waiting slippers, the etiolated arm
tugging a little at a nurse's kindness
though reconciled even to this lost rebellion :
'we come out of the dark and go into the dark again'
as the Hofrat put it in his gently bullying way,
               nothing
of the heated moment lasts and yet nothing
decays. The heart of the storm is now,
God wrecking man on death,
the absurdity of pitching his tone so high—

And the storm-tossed angels
about the bright graveyards and the chimneys
of the Corporation fire-temples,
they have huge albums of memorials,
of Hannah, dearly beloved wife,
of Lieutenant Sanderson, drowned on a boom,
of Grey and Gander, who fell asleep in infancy,
of names unnamed that do not feel
the drip of autumn leaves—
               they know
a barometer from a loving God
but what can they do crouching in His corner?
               Millennia
stop short at three score years and ten
and the only thing on earth which will never
wither away is the state.
               They ask
forgiveness for joking outside your sepulchres;
sometimes the sun shines and it seems
the storm is just a passing thing,
captains of industry smile on white terraces,

the regatta sails like drops of blood
fleck the blue estuary—
                         Back in the Nursing Home
a change on a chart is recorded, the angels
are tossed in its turbulence.
                         Why write poems?
Why, for that matter, march on Moscow
or ask your daughter if she loves you?

The calm. While it lasts, there is man,
and suppose him a creature it's worth
making God for. In that calm, as at Babel,
mercurial masons are singing the truth,
serene diapasons of business and profit,
university judgements, priceless preferments,
courage and cowardice. Perhaps it did happen,
the Renaissance, when even the maggots
had Humanist leanings.
                         The storm will return
but before it claps down on the foreshore
and harbour, put out the lights, the nightlights
and phosphorous and turn the sea upwards
inverting the stars—the long winking banks
are like Mozart or Nature, carrion-joy
that the dumb in the fields pay the price of
and grieve for; a central unfairness
which looks good to the living, loving
on bones of the dead with basset-horns
maundering, and flushed by their faces,
happy as stopwatches, unlectured
by sick-beds or dreams, awaiting
the tempest, the null epicentre.

A STUDY OF A BIRD

With completely retractable sail
he has an ocean surrounding him;
his surface is at all edges
and everywhere the reefs wait
with their yellow surf : he lives
in a cube drawn by a mad artist,
his eyes are along diagonals;
perspective is what we invent
to be like him : he is not like us,
he would never expect an epitaph.

Brave on a tractor while they lunch
he is as vain as a place god,
an inspector of three hundred tall
stalks and the ants' deep shelter.
That sound now—is it the frogs
in their safe swamp, or the crickets
down on their knees? No, it's
the bariolage of useless terror
made by all things born to die—
he dips his head, they are wiping their mouths.

Traction by Leonardo, costume by Audubon,
habitat by John Clare—the Establishment
of creatures chairs him to the top.
There he passes with his flaps down
plumb on a winter tree. We may
take his eggs and measurements
but we cannot levitate. A ring on his leg
will match him to God's census—
only his watching superiors leave
paradise, trailed by a flailing sword.

33

Fields at evening hold the honey
of the sun. He 'fleeth as it were
a shadow', the bird of the Angelus
among the gleaners of Nature :
it is all dark and light to him,
a scene by C. D. Friedrich to us.
Heavier-than-air machine the poet
loves, he overhears these pointless
poignant words : *I am a child of the
Enlightenment, I expect to be happy.*

THREE BAGATELLES

Under the grassed and general earth a space
Of two contending shadows that are still—
This private darkness was a lightness once
Which sinned against its native fantasy,
A hinged desire which swung below the sun
And closed forever : here the words persist—
Your amorous dust is flesh to my chill dust,
Your page of tributes printed on my heart,
I am your resurrection, you my lust,
Lipless, we kiss and never move apart.

*

The unseeing eyes are not within the world,
Their orphic stare is cataracted here.
Of trinities, beauty, love and pleasure
Have faces which philosophers adorn;
The Venus Pudica has two small mouths
But the gale of innocence is not blown out—
A small cadenza on the skin of sex
And see a burning world defy the odds!
Voluptas dies and Caritas will vex,
The gods are loveless, yet they are the gods.

*

Make speed by sloth and give the tortoise wings
As in the perfect day a dead fish floats,
Blood flows from wounds and from the menstrual ditch
The future runs : the childlike lovers age,
War on its knees petitions peaceful love,
A rabble pelts the stricken King of Swans—
The open box of mystery commands
Only such truths as memory puts in.
The eggs of death are warm, futurity stands,
Like the infinity of angels, on a pin.

35

STUDIES FROM LEMPRIÈRE

The Feast of the Gods

In the perfect weather of their soft plateau
The reasonable deities deployed
Their human hungers. What was there more to show
To creatures who never had enjoyed
Freedom from death, but paying with their lives
Bought golden faces, a marble of archives?

It was a pleasure to imagine pain,
The circumstance of love, the stars far out
Which touched them little, and to feel again
That classic innocence when any doubt
Brought wonder to their finished universe,
The tessitura of man's dying curse.

One laid a hand upon his consort's flank
And felt by proxy every warming glance;
Birds of paradise and peacocks shrank
Into the polished fernery; the midday dance
Of animals to please their masters took
A warlike gesture from an open book.

The painter found them at post-prandial games,
Helmets worn askew and breasts exposed,
But having second sight he fed the flames
Of war which lay behind their lovers' pose :
Those long marches were not to any bed
But to the Fields of Fear, the Isle of the Dead.

Not to be moved by misery, not to know
Relish in loving, discontent in age—
Their thoughts were crystalline in sun or snow,
Their history atoms on rampage;
In place of good and bad they had fortune,
An aspect of the clouds and sliding moon.

You see this scene only when very old,
A vision of the unremitting gods
Picknicking as in the Age of Gold,
Not adding to or taking from the odds
But having eternity to live through
Looking beyond the face of death at you.

The Zone of Venus

This was the Attic picture when she drew
Her ribboned waistline to its narrowest.
These things her liberators understood,
The covetable radiance of the New,
Impressive art which might renew the West,
A stranger's touch conferring Neighbourhood.

Her guerdon seemed far otherwise to those
Who entered by the dark sulphurous door;
Would there be light again and would their names
Be heard once more or left beside their clothes
Upon the banks of Hell? Their feet were sore
From running and there were still the Games.

Her daughters found her picture in their hands :
'That was the Sunday night when I was laid
By a man from the Agency.' The goddess turned
To view her imprint in the shining sand—
Where love had been, a grave was freshly made,
Letters were strewn, a votive candle burned.

My darker side, she said, to switch the part,
I have these other gifts, that when I tread
On gorse or waste land, fields of pleasure grow
And this I call the landscape of the heart—
You find that lips can do what you have read,
Words are true, the honeyed anthems flow.

37

But barbarous fate to wake up in a place
Where everything is narrowed into love,
Your tongue her agriculture, war
Between day and night upon her face
And simple sleep murdered from above,
Possession being nine points of the law.

The pictures are deceits, Zephyrus blows
On the nymph's neck to bring up flowers,
Wounded Adonis whistles off his dogs—
Her mischevious girdle on, the goddess goes
Out antlering the world, her playful powers
Serve civil lovers for death's catalogues.

The Descent into Avernus

Coming down from the serious hills upon
The Campanian flatlands, then we saw
The black lake where the stars reflected shone
Among the stagnant argosies of weed,
Small sulphur roses knocking at the shore
And swollen pummice jammed among the reeds.

This was the Leader's promise, a lake without
Birds or any living creature, fanned
By volcanic breath, the home of doubt;
Here we would camp and wait until a sign
Gave presence to the statutory land,
Blood from the earth or voices in a vine.

One of our purposes was to trace the smell,
That all-pervading smell of misery.
Some said it was the heroes dead in Hell
Smothered forever in their victims' flesh,
Others the pus of gods, rot in the Tree
Of Life no mortal creature could refresh.

That it was human where nothing human lived
Was everyone's hypothesis. The shades of armies
Stood behind the midday dazzle, sieved
From a glut of contours by the sun;
Beyond the line of salt some spindly trees
Waved like souls whose torments had begun.

The Leader made survival rules for all—
To be observers of the scene was our
Responsibility. In the long haul
To darkness, man would need supplies,
Rations which the dead could not devour,
Signals beyond his rational faculties.

And so upon the poisoned earth we sat,
The air itself a teeming oracle :
Man's soul might leave him like a cat,
His body come to carbon, yet somewhere
Behind this valley or that clambering hill
He'd find his true and disciplined despair.

DREAMTIME

To the short-of-breath an apotheosis,
To come upstairs behind some Metternich
Of the party-giving world and still be
Recognized; your hostess, her rings shining,
Ready to rescue you out of corners.

This might be the door opening on a dream
Of a prosperous terrain where at last
Scenery germane to the heart is displayed :
Silos with clocks, the Norman church deaf
To the procession with the lilied corpse,

Half-Cockaigne among the seaweed grasses
And the animal moon awake all day,
Severe streets opening suddenly after fields
Of grain, the calm citizens ambling through
Huzzahs of troops for a near-sighted heir;

The parturition of the Princess golden
With balconies, and the revolutionaries' smithy
Watched by a bored spy; melancholy hours
In the cafés without even a betrayal
Or a sexual touch of foot or finger.

That is the scene, but it may change.
We may hurry to some Horatian outhouse
For the evening reading and discourse blood
On the pink-faced terrace, someone nearby
Playing the flute at a lizard listening.

Hate in the hills where the rebels practise
Games with black gourds, boredom in the library
At any time of day, but fear always,
Fear in everything. Responsibility for this
Is the question on each person's tongue.

They will try to get you to dream a new world
For them, one made clean by courage. You
May need to give a hostage as you do now
When you see approaching the perennial bore
Who is host to nature and a lord of change.

MEANWHILE

Doch unverständig ist
Das Wünschen vor dem Schicksal.
Die Blindesten aber
Sind Göttersöhne.

Hölderlin.

The source of all things is in themselves
but there must be pictures to hang in Heaven—
       the whale flensed in a chalky sea
       to make a dawn;
       craters of the afternoon
under eaves of the Fichtelgebirge;
       a mouth patrolling
a million eggs knowing its time will come.
       Simplicity, complexity
       and the words between !
Such pretty critics of our carelessness—
       what if we say
'I have tried to give up abstracts
but I cannot tell a laurel leaf
from a collar stiffener.'
       The soul
might look out through the eyes if only
all incoming traffic ceased a while.
       Till then, judicious murder.
Ruins run the landscape. Lodges
of Unlikeliness where dickering birds
inspirit sundials, a chequerboard
of turf above Moravian sleepers,
love leaving and arriving through
a gangster's ganglia, and then that music
which asks an amnesty of death.
       Mixed feelings
no less than metaphors.

The wickedest dream
man ever dreamed
showed him to himself
as pure spirit :
we live still in the horror of it.
The gods come tumbling
to repair the damage, flattering us
with little evils—
a sculpture of snot
and Daphne's earwax,
payola for the trumpeting
of blood, the carcass
of a tear.

This riddling tone
is for the fierce enthusiasts and drumming
critics : theirs is the lust of change,
the module of imagination, but instead
we enjoy and through eternity
a breakfast after dreaming.
In the German
Meanwhile we lie down with words,
shaped into silence or thronging
to accuse. Our only health
is to be moved by movers, hearing
in stark quiet the order to conduct
the once-living through our lives.
This lifts the gods
from grovelling
at mortal spoor
and faces them
with loneliness and blind amenity.

DOWN CEMETERY ROAD

The wind brings the Sunday bells. Come to church
good people. But for me they're simulacra
of the great bell in my chest, clouting out the end.

This comes of keeping one's nose to the moral north
where gods go when they die. Oh how pleased
they are to leave their Babylonian captivity.

And how strange that religion comes from the East
where tourists see only commerce—fanaticism
seeking blue-eyed converts in the claggy fens.

But not the point of this poem. The chorale of Bach's
which moves me most is a tune of 1713,
a real contemporary, *Liebster Gott, wann wird ich sterben?*

The tune is Daniel Vetter's, the treatment Bach's.
There's the soft flush of earth when corpse and men
move among the mattutinal flowers.

Bells like teeth touching, the towers of Leipzig
carving a Lutheran world in friendly slices,
that warm sententiousness we know as death.

Almost chirpy music, but don't ask the corpse
his view. Perhaps he sees that transcendental
radish bed promised by the tame Tibetans.

After a lifetime of blood letting, we deserve
a vegetable future. The flutes and oboes pilfer grief,
we have earned this joyful gruesomeness.

I think I was six when first I thought of death.
I've been religious ever since. Good taste
lay in wait and showed me avenues of music.

Which opened on the road to Leipzig's cemetery,
the alder trees in leaf and the choristers
waiting for their dinner. *Herrscher über Tod und Leben!*

We Northerners are really Greek. Stoic, old
and held by oracles. Tears are running down like soot.
My daily prayer, *Mach einmal mein Ende gut!*

A TOCCATA OF MUFFAT'S

The Herr Burgomeister is mining his teeth. Keep pressure
Up in all the bourgeois organs, this is God's sanity,
    Blowing air at calibrated lengths,
    Voiding Heaven for South Germany.

You will die not young, nor very old, but dusty on top :
Pleasures in the Palmengarten, the brass taste of logic
    And the graveyards holding a pedal
    For the repeated Fs of Jesus.

Darkness and the smell of wax snuffed out! *Zum Grünen Anker*
Where they ride on seas of blond wine, tasting self like sugar—
    The masked hours moused by my fat cat
    With all of Sunday to come home to !

It is forever before the cataclysm, hermits
Are boiling the state, but one gentle mad poet discounts
    The *furor teutonicus* with swan-
    polished sails on the Swabian dusk.

Tiptoe through the granaries and old lead workings—
This is the bridgework of a Protestant Book of Beauty,
    The flowers Luther leered at, types of
    Forgiveness for aunts and abbatoirs.

Being translated into pretty Music Programme vowels,
A morning canto for Anglo-Saxon reasonableness—
    The thundering of bells overhead,
    The rendering of praise overheard.

Storm cones, conical icons of the middle element,
Hang like mad sausages in the organ-builder's brain-box,
    A wind to swell out Dorotheas
    And cool our diary-keeping cousins.

46

Witches are baking, hares sleeping in the stubble, ravens,
Black, unglücklich, cawing for the chance of further mischief;
       Now time is turned to drops of music,
       Apollo on *Posaune* and *Gedackt.*

The pebble in the stream is run from by the sun. Listen!
One is one and all alone and evermore shall be so.
       The air is arguing with itself,
       The gods are in the room, eavesdropping.

CAT'S FUGUE

What a clever moggie to tread only
    in the keys of G Minor and D Minor,
but then the gifted walk with care and flair
    as if on hot bricks; their bloodless
sleepwalking looks like exodus
    and the daggers are such dashing
footnotes. I chatted up a puss about Scarlatti
    but he had his Mason's secrets
and all I got was whiskers. Worthy men
    were walking by the gothic tulips,
sparrows purloined ears, so obviously
    the world was wired for sound.
Before you make your poem seem too twee
    I'll warn you, said the cat,
it's knowing when to stretto, how to keep
    your counter-subjects simple,
what to do when grandeur blows your mind—
    also, you'll notice that my fur
lies one way, so please don't brush it backwards
    and call the act experiment.
That sour cat was dead against our century
    and I was so ambitious,
I bought a cosmological notebook,
    Zinoviev's new machine
and a glossary of the German terms in Joyce—
    I'm in retirement till I make
my violent masterpiece; it's about a cat
    bigger than Bulgakov's, east
of Jeoffry in the night sky of the Lord;
    it stalks like plague along the grass
fathering history on the post-diluvial age—
    named Jesus at the whole Jerusalem,
the Day of Modernism dawns; professors touched
    by wings fly purring to the moon.

These are its juvenilia and in Horatian
      retrospect I see the cat
restored to its domestic stalking one salt
      Iberian morning in the light
when genius saddened at the cold keyboard
      is jacked with white and black—
again our dainty-footed man's companion
      strikes a balance with the dust
and props the world against its weary gravity.

THE SETTEMBRINI WALTZ

Time was, the fund of knowledge
Led to the barricades
And not, as in this college,
To making higher grades.

That was the great Cenacle
When dew formed in the night
Would coruscate and sparkle
On police boots polished bright.

When pages out of Balzac
And things the Fathers wrote
Were more than some Old Pals Act
Or urban guerilla's quote.

But polish up your Fanon
And keep your Brechtwerk gay,
The latest sine qua non
Is Ethnic Shadowplay.

Hearing the Appassionata
Sapped Lenin's will to fight,
But Cage's cool self-starter
Sits squadrons down to write.

Let's end it one cold morning
With bullets in a bed,
All ironies self-scorning
And liberal Europe dead.

PRINT OUT: APOCALYPSE

When the army of ecologists
has scraped the last shellfish
from the lagoon,

When all the cars on
the urban overpasses are towed
to adventure playgrounds,

When the phrase 'fossil fuel'
is considered too holy to be used
in crossword puzzles,

When Thirties hats and hairdos
have come back into fashion
for the tenth time,

When archivists have stored
reserve prints of every manifestation
of popular culture,

When software and hardware
have swapped places in our
advanced computers,

When these words are fed in
for me to consider, I will come again,
says the Lord . . . .

BAROQUE QUATRAINS DEDICATED TO JAMES FENTON

Morning Song of a Court Dwarf

Dollops of iodine ease the fuming king
As De Guzman tells her maid to lace her tighter,
Epic lapdogs treadle on a swing,
The fountains' susurring grown still politer.

Organ pipes are cradled in a skull
To stall the clouds above the ferrous plain;
Our new tientos are obscene and dull,
The roof of Paradise lets in the rain.

The War of Widows buzzes somewhere off.
Sophistication leaves court etiquette to
The portrait painters: the Infanta's killing cough
Halts bald kanakas at their war canoe.

Ambassadors of northern countries stand
Impassive while our hierophants intone
Long canticles of Christ the Contraband:
Our grandees' hearts are shrunk to kidney stones.

To every morning task its discipline—
Some to make our skyscraper sorbetti,
Others gazump the price of prunes, and in
The boat all Europe waving from the jetty.

Death of a Comic Opera Composer

Balmoral balconies are tossed in gloom;
The short-lived whimper at a world which needs
Soap and some psalming. 'I like a billiard room,
The National Geographical Magazine, nasturtium seeds.'

Nonsense has corners, has a sense of focus,
Especially when the entracte thumps too long,
I say the magic names, *Keeling or Cocos,*
Esarhaddon, Klopstock, Suzie Wong.

Don't let a stanza come between your God
And you, and don't rely on stale *Rossiniana,*
The Music Critic who is not a sod
Can't black a knuckle at 'the grand pianner'.

Enough of dicing, playing 'crack the finger'
With Mephisto inside *Le Père-Lachaise,*
All men must feed their balls into the wringer
However few or many are their days.

The light is fading, randy darkness waits;
I am inviolate, 'grâce à mon plongeon'—
Those beaks above the bed, are they the Fates?
Tell Death I'm not a man to mix his genres.

The Queer Assayers of the Frontier

Our scene shifts to a Hunting Lodge in which
A clutch of pretty primpers is on points;
Doubtless we'll breakfast in the tombs, the rich
Are so macabre—cold plovers' eggs, veal joints

And liquorice lollies, sitting by cadavers—
The band has brought its timbrels and the boys
Are melancholy thinking of lifesavers
On Palermo beach and other departed joys.

The provinces are either wet and wild
Or dusty and disgusting—boarding houses
Full of loud galoots, their bathrooms tiled
With funny fishes, hung with dripping blouses.

If I weren't sick, I'd leap upon my donkey
And leave this place for good; if I had cash
I'd buy a cliffside villa with a wonky
Punkah and Solarium—I'd have a bash

At beating Claudian at his panegyric,
The Classic and the Christian at a blow,
Take nights off at the *Roxy* and the *Lyric*
And watch the ferry chuntering to and fro.

EPIGRAMS OF THE ABBOT BŪ-SHOU-SĒ

When the eyelid falls, weed drifts upwards
on the wheel of lakes. A louse crawling
on a corpse feels the onset of an Ice Age.
Pavilions of birds enclose the Emperor's bride.

Calm men wonder in vermilion glare
how the web-foot creature finds its love.
Today the bath of oracles, the lotus hinge,
thirty-one words to base your life upon.

Dreams—the Theatre of Chaos.
Life—the Theatre of Action.
Art—the Theatre of Order.
Death—the Theatre of Reality.

Records are women,
they have their holes in the middle.
These are the ones you never played,
they're setting up secondaries in the corridor.

The bright face of the clock is set for silence
or the sooner bang. Applaud the rice for having stood
so long. Of death, discipline and the sparrow's eye,
the sage has one requirement—wait!

Put your ear to a tombstone, the crying
never stops. Our adept is past the fifth door.
The philosopher 'Cabbage Ears' never tired
of the pattern on his carpet. The sixth door shuts.

Among the clean tributaries we found the octave.
Their fallen Winter Gardens show they had
a way of notating heaven. 'God, a yellow bean,
The Adversary, fruit between the legs.'

55

'Tum Tum' offered to divert a river for us
but we were not prepared for luck. Collecting
honey, I met her by the gate. She stung me
as I played with her. *Revolvit lapidem.*

I was coming home by the short cut through
the woods when I heard a different bird
inside my head. Immediately, I had the words,
'Who sandpapers the world is God, is God.'

Our religion has no Calvary
but we are hung
on a cross
by death.

Most of the penances to hand—
Insulin, ECT, Aversion Therapy—
Are nothing to the man who knows
he is commanded to eat his God.

EXIT, PURSUED BY A BEAR

Others abide our question. Thou art free.
Art not an artist but an industry,
And to a nation fallen on hard times
Worth more than North Sea Oil or Yorkshire Mines:
Indeed, our Bardic Tours and Shakespeare Tomes,
With the Royal Family, Scotch and Sherlock Holmes,
Convince the U.S.A. and E.E.C.
That though we're not what once we used to be
If there's some sale which needs a bit of class
An English accent's all that you can ask—
Our actors, raised on Bolingbroke and York,
Can hold their own at late-night TV talk,
Directors trained by England's classic teachers
Bring something more to Ads. and Second Features,
And poet-dons, with ear and taste defective,
On sixteenth-century love life turn detective,
Track amorous ladies with Italian looks
Through sonnets, diaries, letters and part-books—
Our GNP, from Inverness to Flatford,
Could take a hint from tourist-battered Stratford;
An asset nursed need never be depleted,
The English Language cannot be defeated.

We owe this to the man for whom we're here,
Our Superstar, our J.C., our Shakespeare,
And if one's heart sinks in the London Library
Or trying to work the BM without bribery
Confronted with the Shakespeare section looming
Above us like a ship's hull (that's assuming
This metaphor impresses jet-age readers)
The mind, that most debased of dirty feeders,
Is more than pleased to see four hundred years
Of parasitic comment raised in tiers,
Unsought, unread, uncared-for and undusted,

The whole life's work for which dead men once lusted,
Grabbed office, wheedled, schemed and struggled through,
Reduced to Nothing after Much Ado!
But exegesis lives and dies, it's not
(Whatever you may think, you clan of Kott)
The point: we've got the plays in fine editions,
We know interpolations and additions,
And may, setting scholarship among the sins then,
Say Shakespeare wrote *The Two Noble Kinsmen*—
At least the very best bits, and then stretch a
Point and reassign to worthy Fletcher
All that tedious play, *King Henry the Eighth*,
Like Wolsey's bladders, not much puffed of late.
While praising Shakespeare, let us not forget
Contemporaries who left us in their debt,
Those men whom Swinburne praised in Mermaid dress—
The more of Middleton's is not the less
Of Shakespeare's glory and *The Broken Heart*
If not quite *Antony* is stunning art.
May they receive as many new productions
As teenage Romeos their set seductions
(See Martin Amis's *The Rachel Papers*
For the latest slant on young love cutting capers):
Let all the kudos this great name has stored
Be used to recommend the plays of Ford.

But now, alas, I reach the nasty part
Of this encomium—dramatic art
Is only half alive upon the page;
What then of Shakespeare on the modern stage?
I've sat through *Troilus* in the Second Empire,
Lear in local government, 'one that gathers samphire,
Dreadful trade', but surely not of Dover's
Since Edgar's dressed to play for Bristol Rovers;
Macbeth in trench coats and his guilty Lady
Somnambulizing fully-frontal, Brady

And Hindley to the life, as if the Bard
Were playing understudy to de Sade—
Then *Hamlet* 'en risotto', lines all diced
And dished up like a bowl of savoury rice—
Still, none of this is quite as bad as what
TV has done—sans time, sans lines, sans plot,
Sans everything but window dressing, got
Through with much relief : since money's time
The classics on the box can be a crime.
Then there's Shakespeare politicized by Brecht,
Hung-up by Brook, portrayed by Bond and wrecked
In any one of twenty thousand ways—
The mortal genius of some thirty plays,
Whose 'lives' as Mr. Schoenbaum rightly says
Are many as a cat's, since each enhancer
Sees him like himself, a necromancer,
A Catholic, a crypto-queer, a Cornish Warlock
(He only lacks his own 'Person from Porlock'),
But always there behind that Stratford bust
Or in those undug feet of common dust
The Grand Enigma of each generation,
Surviving even fashion and translation,
And like his favourite Ovid ever changing
Gods and Men in Nature, rearranging
The world we others fancy is opaque,
Or cannot understand or simply fake
Until it seems Creation's paradigm,
A timeless dream which yet unfolds in time.

I'll finish now this commonplace recital
By just explaining why I chose its title—
It's from, of course you know, *The Winter's Tale* :
The man the bear rended tooth and nail
Was loyal Antigonus, the child Perdita,
One of the nicest heroines by far,
Too good to serve up as an ursine entrée—

59

But think, the man who put her in the play
Had daughters of his own, and how did he
Treat them, his wife, his son, his family?
One fact alone I dare to say tonight,
Shakespeare's younger daughter couldn't write,
Her mark is on some document, a cross—
Imagination must be at a loss
To think his mind, though blackened by his spouse's,
Cared less for daughters than for Stratford houses!
It opens up the way for royal Lear,
An avenue of anger lit by fear—
The bear is death which chases him so long
And never can be quietened with a song,
Each creature of the plays a funeral mute
Lamenting Orpheus and his broken lute,
And on some dismal shore the bones are cracked,
The genius of the universe ransacked.